A Beautiful Body

Michael David Rigney

Copyright © 2017 by Michael David Rigney

All rights reserved. This book or any portion thereof may not be reproduced or used in any manner whatsoever without the express written permission of the publisher except for the use of brief quotations in a book review.

Printed in the United States of America

ISBN-13: 978-1979967174
ISBN-10: 1979967172

For more information about the author please visit his personal website at www.digitaloutsider.com.

To view the author's visual artworks made available for purchase online, please visit www.printpop.com/MikeR2869.

The author's first book of poems is available on Amazon www.amazon.com/Enigma-Michael-David-Rigney/dp/0982858760.

A Beautiful Body | Michael David Rigney

Dedicated to all of the Roses in the world....

As an artist, my greatest inspiration comes from interactions with various types of people. I wander through the world documenting the experiences and emotions that result from an emotionally open observation of life. An observation where judgement is suspended and, in its place, is a raw view of the myriad forms that comprise humanity.

This book especially is the result of that sort of work. Here I have taken on the most commonly held ideas of beauty and the resulting diminishing sense of self that seems to come with them. It is my hope and dream that this small book makes a difference in someone else's life.

For me, this writing process has been a challenge to see beyond the self-destructive nature of how women often view their bodies and suggest an alternate view that is far less self-destructive. With that said, I hope you enjoy this book....

How **beautiful** a body...
What is it **worth** to you???

Do you mean to spell it out
    by just how much you care about
        the people *whom you choose* to give it to?

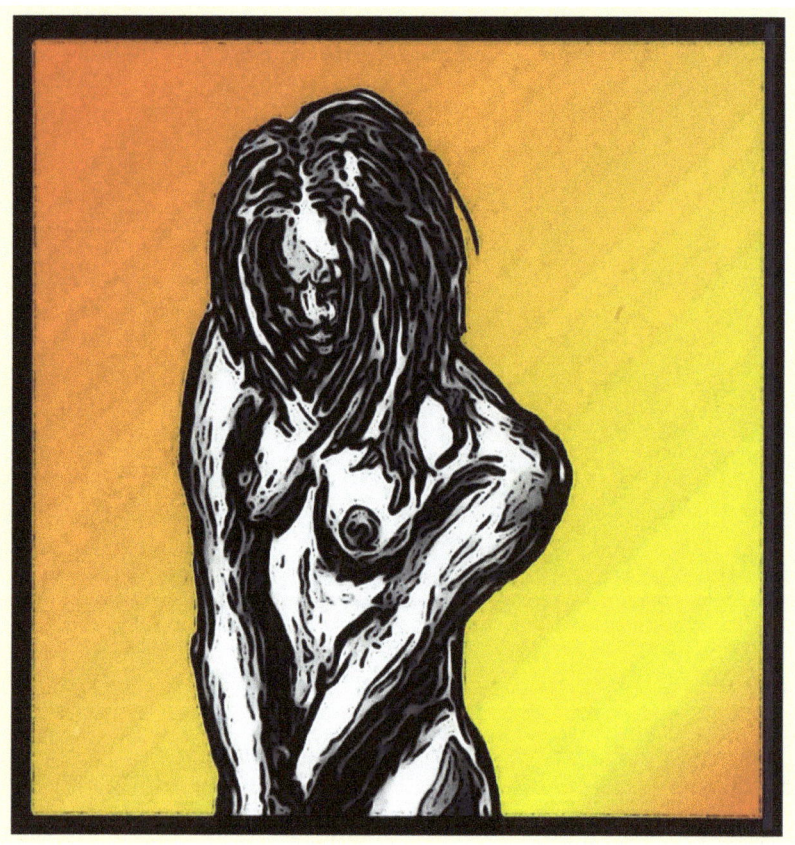

As I
found her

    Tragic,
    really

A life
    that entered
        mine...

A girl of sorts
who did not find

herself to be
    so *pretty,*
        or desirably
            refined...

But who, it seemed,
had started to
in very recent times...

And so **I found her**
being pretty

In her body;
spread around
quite quickly

By a self
that's **seen**
as beautiful

When a
    beautiful **self**
        resounds...

Based mostly in
the common bounds

That **beauty is desired**

And not merely
    something *found*....

There is no *sense*
In **what she does**...

No *meaningful direction*
To her **lust**...

Blindly *blowing kisses*
In the **dark**...

She will take *anyone*
Who **asks the part**...

The faulted actions
Of her dealings

By her *unknown*
In real **feelings**...

You see...

To her so-called
Husband,
An **object**;
His to own

A piece of *property*
In **his home**

There is no *sense*
In her **senseless acts**

Because her husband
Broke her back...

She only *wanted*
To be **seen**

And did not *intend*
To be **unclean**...

She thought
That the takers
Of the part

Somehow could *see*
Her **broken heart**...

But she was **mistaken**
And she *shrank*
Each time her **dignity**
Was *taken*

While all that she got
In exchange
For her heart's
Plea

Were the takers
Of the part

Who could not
Really *see*
Her **heart**...

Eying herself,
longing
madly in the **dark**...
a self-perception
lowly and **stark**;
a wanting
misconception
of a beautiful *spark*...

When a self is seen
as undesirable,
unwanted and in need...
in a tragic
course of actions,
the heart
can **manifest**
misdeed

When she
stares
into a *mirror*,
the **beauty**
that's there found
is *colored* in **deception**
by the *dissonant sound*
of a hundred myriad **abuses**

ringing out at once,

blinding her
to what the truth is,
not allowing her
to see
that she
is *beautiful*,
priceless,
a *miracle*
to behold,

unlike
the jaded image
of the **lies**
that she
was told

And so she goes
in her misperception,
grabbing on to anyone
who desires her *attention*,
giving freely satisfaction
in a dehumanizing,
impersonal
physical
action

Another self-dilution,
another planted seed,
taking her **heart** further
from any *absolution*
of the longing
she's conceived

Mistaking **lust**
for *beauty*;
mistaking
love
for *greed*;
leaving her **heart**
hurting
and her **soul**
in *need*....

I don't need to tell you
what it means to me...

To **know** yourself
instead of *hiding*
would change
the world,
you see...

Really, I can tell you
that **life** or **death** is *love*,
and that the heart's
attentive care
is worth the **pain**
of letting loose
your numbing,
hiding
glove...

To sit and stare
into a **mirror**
and *see* without
the **lies**

Believing in the *miracle*
that's **windowed** by your *eyes*...

Well, that alone
will quell the **fear**

And *clear* the **curses**
that deafen your ear

Letting **truth**
you'd rather hear
be *sounded* out again...

Sounding now the same, it does
as it sounded when it was
a *doubtless* life **conviction**

Before you were
the **victim**....

If you saw *yourself*
    as I do

It would not be hard to see
    the truth that you are **beautiful**
        and *valued* immensely

If you saw *yourself*
    as I do

Then your heart would show **clearly**,
    and the truth that you are *loveable*
        would then be seen by you
            as it is seen by me

If you saw *yourself*
    as I do

You would be *set free,*
    and thoughts of your low **value**
        would *vanish* instantly

And if you saw *yourself*
    as I do

You would then *agree*
    with the fact that you are **priceless**
        and truly *seen to be*

But only if you saw *yourself*
    as I do

For whenever I take time to *look*,
it is **clear** to me....

A Beautiful Body | Michael David Rigney

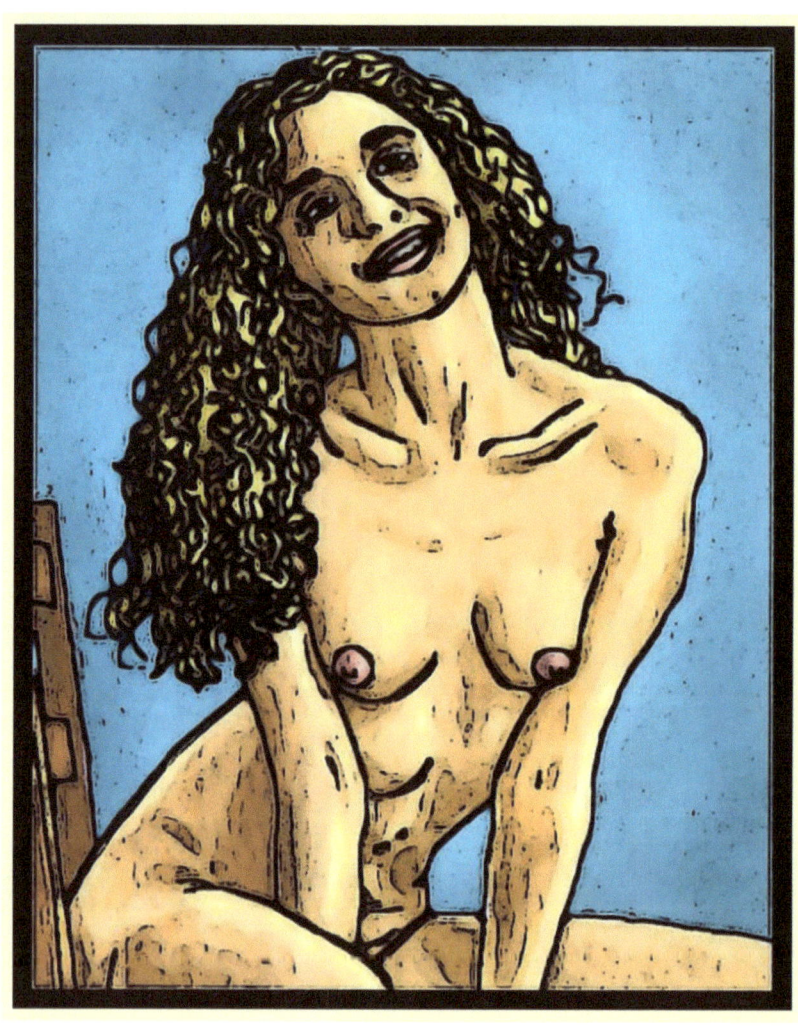

To *love* is not a **choice**,
    Though *loving* a **decision**

Expressed in
    Parting life

As **love**
    Of self
        Self-given

By the **value**
    Of *decisions*

Made in *choices*
    Life is **lived** in

That show
    The **love**
        Of self

Uniquely from
    Within them....

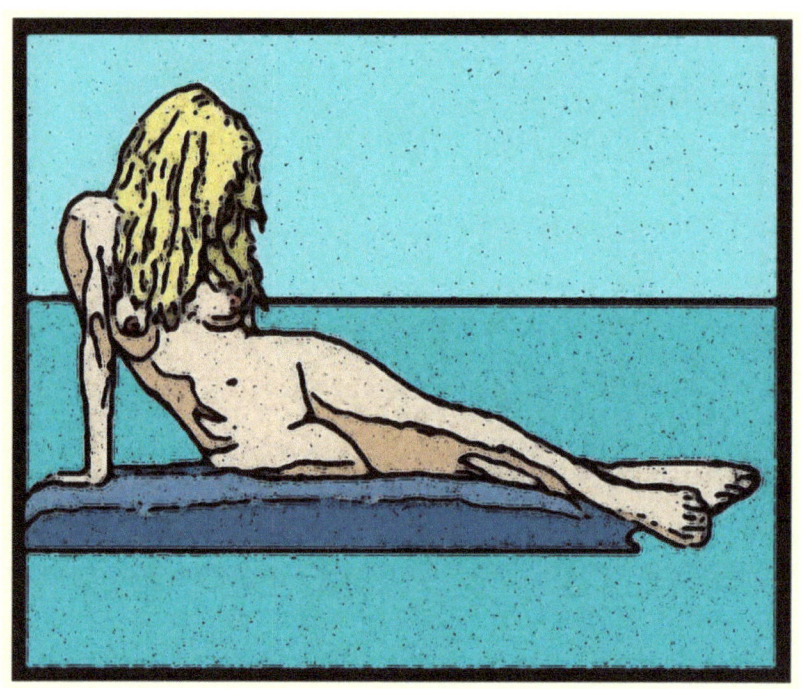

What is it that becomes of you
when the **value** of yourself
is **pathologically** *objectified*
into an impersonal being,
only *valued* for a **function**
to *give* **satisfaction**,
which you grant
by your action
for any defined
literal expression
of *desire*
as **intention**...?

A Beautiful Body | Michael David Rigney

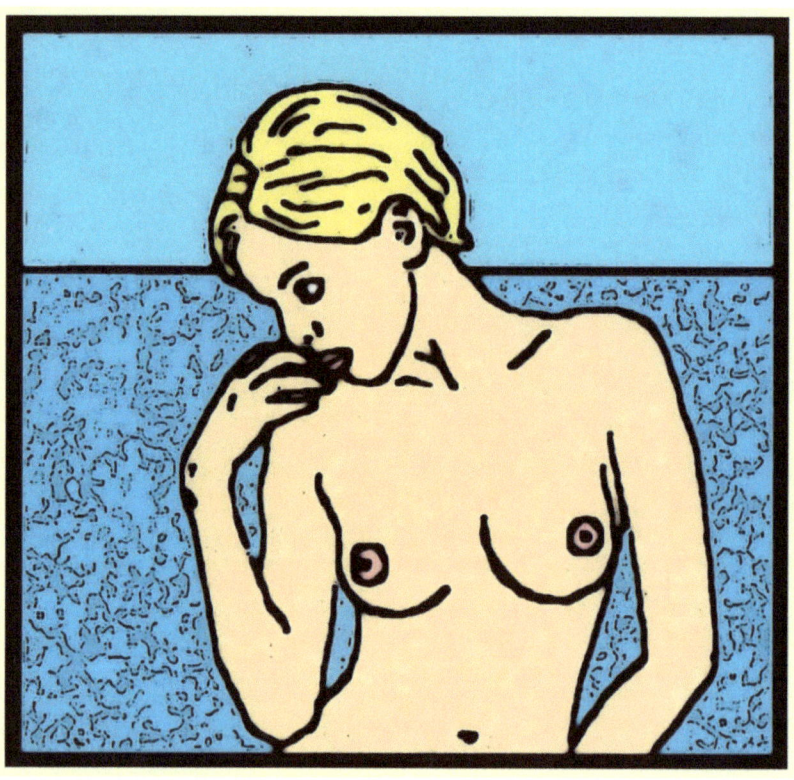

I *only wanted*
 to **feel** *wanted*,
she said

I *wanted* in some **need**

I only *wanted* to **feel** *loved*
 Like the feathers of a dove

I am sorry that it **hurt** me,
 to *fill* his **lustful greed**

I am sorry for my body
 being *used*
and my **longing**
 brought-out
  deed....

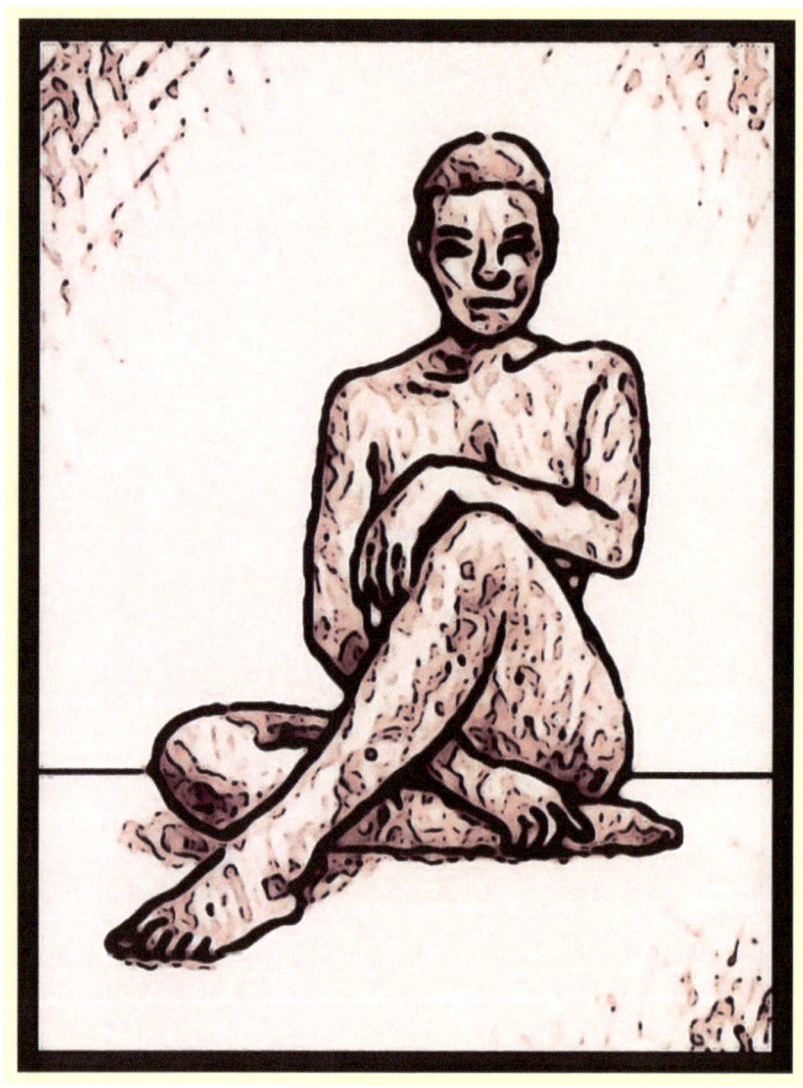

The **hardships**
That you dealt with
In your *coming of age*
Left you *living* your life
As if *trapped*
In a **cage**

Wanting only a **dream**
But *given* **nightmares**
Your **heart**,
It *grew* **darker**;
Entrapped
In **despair**

A bond of *spoken* **love**
Turned into **abuse**...
Your hardships
That you dealt with
As an **object** of *use*

They left you
So senseless,
So reckless
And **blind**
With only
Desires
Left
On your
Mind

And the **hardships**
That you dealt with
Had you *living* them out
In actions
So **loveless**,
Carelessly
Flung about....

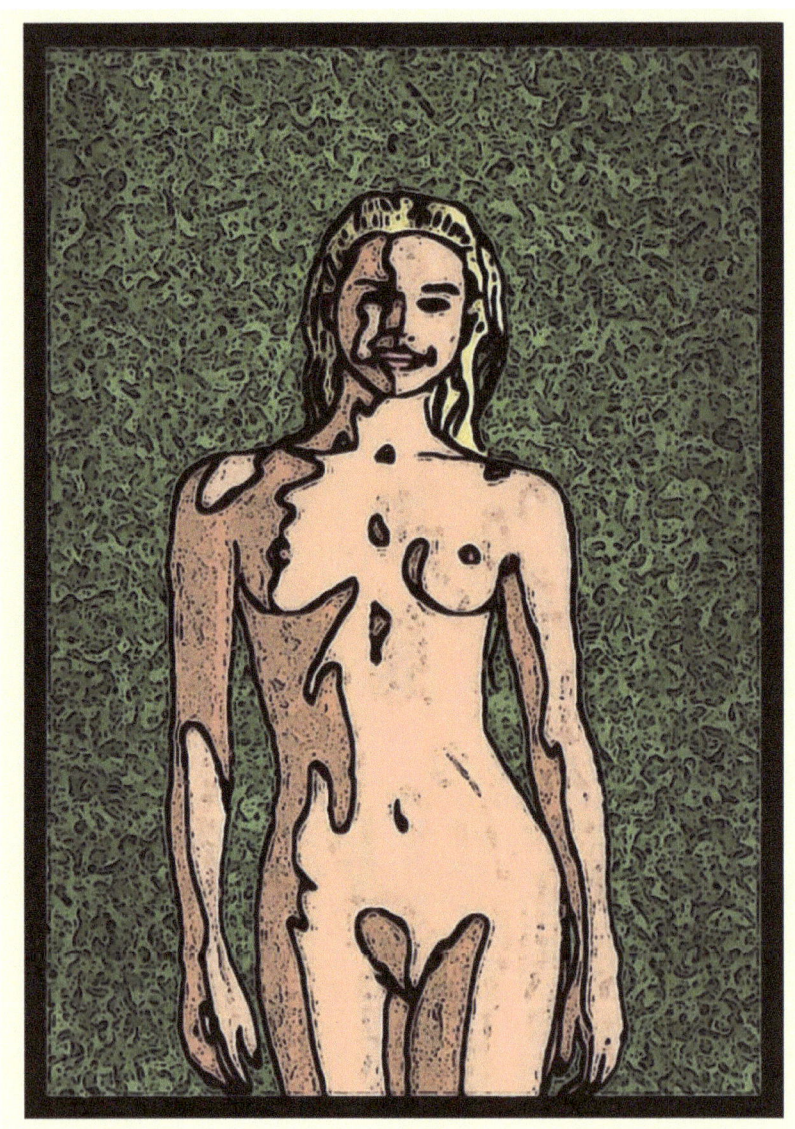

A Beautiful Body | Michael David Rigney

I know that I will *reach* you
    and *see* you where **you are**...

For since the day I *found* you
    in a **form** not as *you are*

You've grown **visible**
    more *clearly*

Yet still seen
    from afar

As *passing* **days**
    show by your ways

The **person**
    that *you are*

I *see* you
    ever closer

Leading me
    to one day **be**

Placed by **time**
    of *passing*

As **close** enough,
    then finally

To *see* you where **you are**....

A Beautiful Body | Michael David Rigney

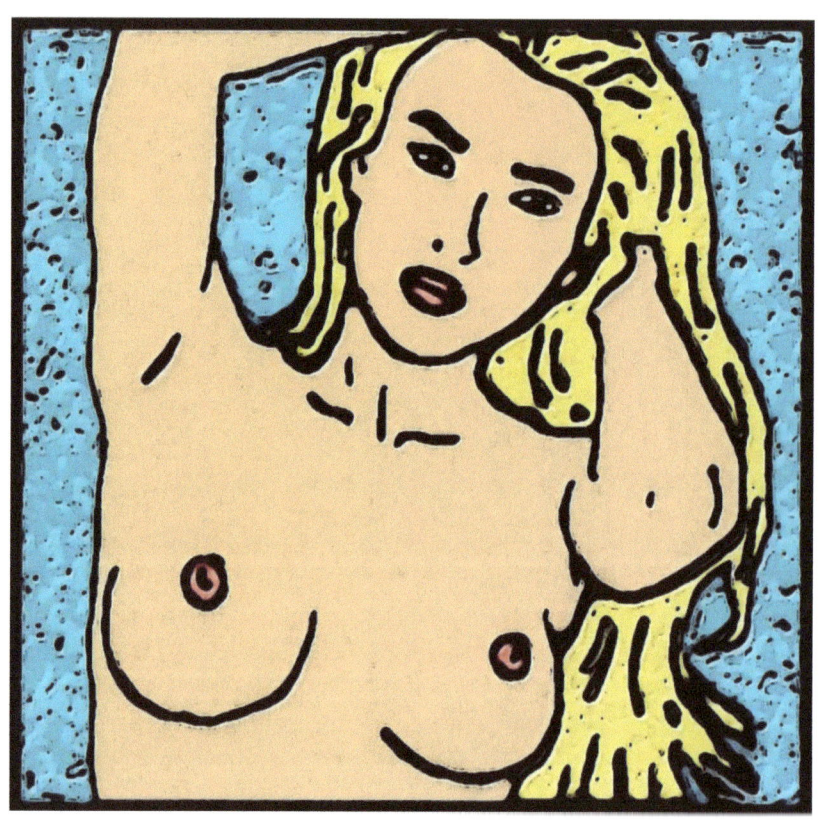

A **dream** becoming *real*...

With each new metric *pulse*,

A **blip** of *actualization*,

Manifesting the heart's **desires**

In a **procession** of *tiny* **glimpses**...

Revealing in time as **whole**,

The true *unbroken* **spirit**

That is the **human** *soul*....

A Beautiful Body | Michael David Rigney

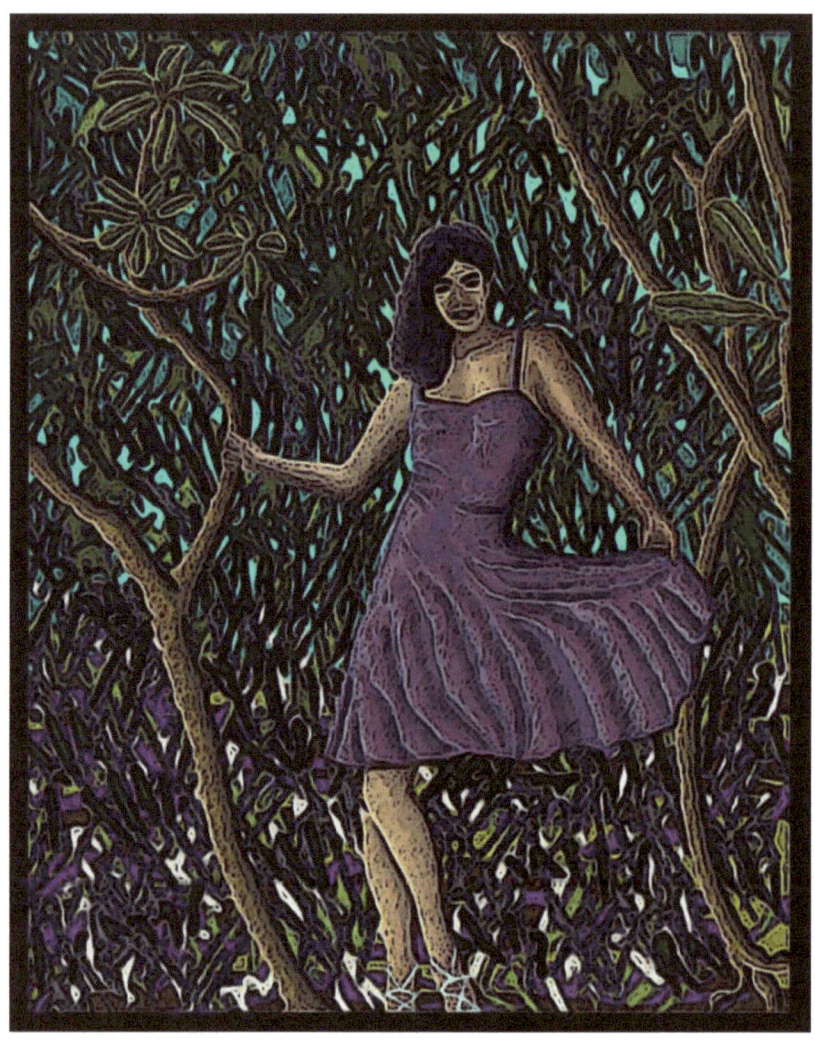

Know that you are *priceless*
Of **worth** *beyond* all gold

And *see* within **yourself**
The **beauty** clearly shown

By the *unique* **heart**
Whose beating
Is entirely **your own**

Both *beautiful*
And **lovely**

More **precious**
Than *measures*
Known...

See the **beauty**
Of yourself

Found **in you**
When **truly** *seen*

Having **beauty** absolute
Not granted by *desiring*

As is clearly shown
Within the true

Uniquely **beautiful**
You....

A Beautiful Body | Michael David Rigney

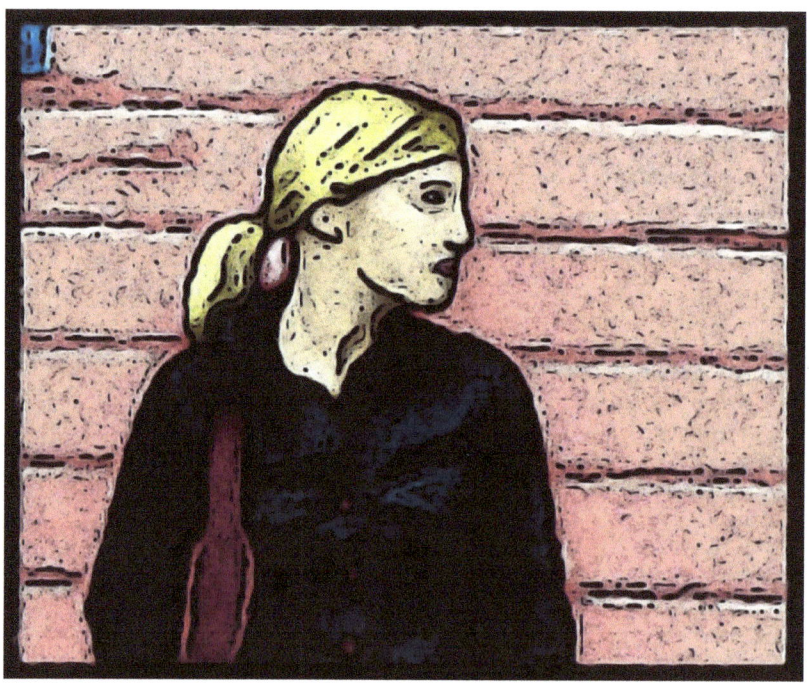

It must have been *divine*
After life had left her blind
And lost in **darkness**

She felt the *pain*
Of her actions
And when I met her
I felt the same

She was
In her heart *diminished*
And needing **healing**

But in that **darkness**
There was a *light*
Ever *brighter*
Than the **night**

And though her heart
At first was bleeding,
The *light*, she followed
By its leading

And from the **pain**,
She gained respite;
Her heart a *freedom*
From its **plight**

And she was led
By course of *time*
Into **daybreak**,
Redefined....

A Beautiful Body | Michael David Rigney

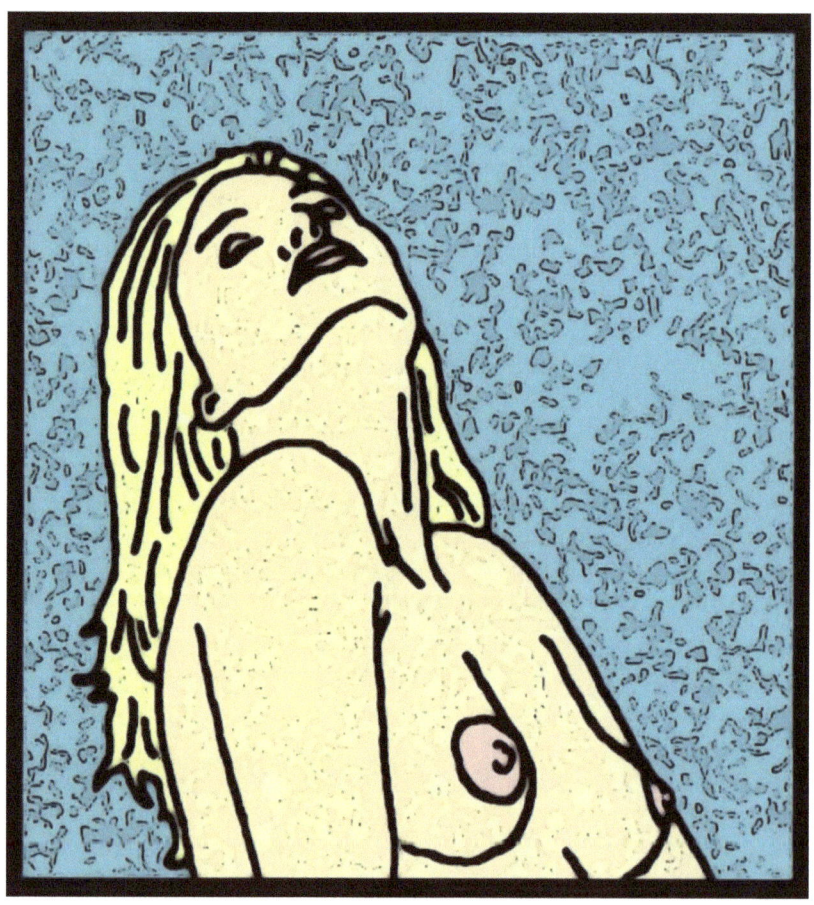

Deep in my **heart**,
    I *uphold* the stance

That **life** should be *lived*
    Like a *mad* **romance**

A *passionate* you
    In all that **you do**

A *passion* for **life**
    For a *passionate* **few**....

Fin.

www.ingramcontent.com/pod-product-compliance
Lightning Source LLC
Chambersburg PA
CBHW040255220526
45473CB00001B/485